BIRTHDAY FUN

Kingfisher

NEW YORK

KINGFISHER
Larousse Kingfisher Chambers Inc.
95 Madison Avenue
New York, New York 10016

First edition 1995
2 4 6 8 10 9 7 5 3
Copyright © Larousse plc 1995

LIBRARY-OF-CONGRESS CATALOGING-IN-PUBLICATION DATA
Randall, Ronne.
Birthday fun / written by Ronne Randall;
illustrated by Annabel Spenceley.—1st American ed.
p. cm.
1. Birthday fun—Juvenile literature. 2. Children's parties—
Juvenile literature. 1. Spenceley, Annabel, ill. II. Title.
GV1472.7.B5R36 1995
793.2'1–dc20 94-27006 CIP AC

Edited by Nancy Bliss
Designed by Brian Robertson

ISBN 1-85697-548-7

Printed in Hong Kong

Contents

Welcome to Birthday Fun!

Your birthday is the most special day of the year—almost like your own personal holiday! So you want to celebrate it in the most enjoyable way possible. Birthday Fun will tell you everything you need to know to make your next birthday the best one ever.

Most people celebrate with a party, and you'll find party ideas galore in this book. But you don't need to have a party to enjoy most of the activities. Just decide which ones you'd like to try, get some friends together—and have a barrel of birthday fun!

A party or get-together is more fun if it has a theme. A theme will also help you plan games, activities, and food. There's no limit to the themes you can choose—create your own zoo with an animal party, take to the seas with a pirate party, or have a Hollywood party, complete with Oscars!

Party Themes

Hurrah for Hollywood!

If you love movies, be a superstar with a Hollywood party! You and your friends can dress up as your favorite actors, or come as directors or scriptwriters. If someone can video the party, even better! At the end, award chocolate "Oscars" for the best performances in party games.

Party Animals

You and your friends can dress up as animals—and have a great time stalking in your backyard jungle. Or grab your cutlass, hoist the Jolly Roger, and have a swashbuckling pirate party. On the next few pages you'll find out how to make costumes for these and other terrific theme parties.

You will need
construction paper • scissors • glue or cellophane tape • ribbon or yarn • paints and brushes • face paints • adhesive tape

Elephant

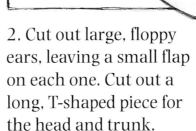

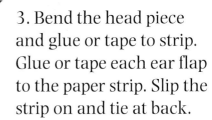

1. Cut a paper strip to fit around your face. Stick together as shown. Attach yarn to tie around the back of your head.

2. Cut out large, floppy ears, leaving a small flap on each one. Cut out a long, T-shaped piece for the head and trunk.

3. Bend the head piece and glue or tape to strip. Glue or tape each ear flap to the paper strip. Slip the strip on and tie at back.

Lion

Cut fringes in a long strip of paper. Tape ends together to fit around your face. Add a nose and whiskers with face paint.

Rhino

Fold and trim paper as shown. Tape together at ends. Cut out holes for eyes, and add horns and ears.

Giraffe

Make face as shown. Make a tube for the neck, attach face, and add ears, horns, and yarn to tie under your chin. Paint on spots!

Ahoy There, Matey!

Hat: Cut two matching hat shapes out of black paper. Fasten together securely. Draw a skull and crossbones on white paper, cut out, and glue to front of hat.

Beard: Use face paints or cut out of felt.

Belt: Cut a wide band of felt. Glue on a cardboard buckle painted gold or silver.

Boots: Add cardboard cuffs to an ordinary pair of black boots.

Monster Bash

You will need
garbage bag • balloons • tape • felt-tip pens • yarn • stretchy headband • construction paper • pair of old gloves

1. Turn the garbage bag upside-down and cut out a hole for your head and two holes for your arms.

2. With a friend's help, tape the balloons to the garbage bag. Be as zany as you can with shapes and colors!

3. Cut eyelashes out of construction paper and tape them to two (or three!) balloons to make the eyes.

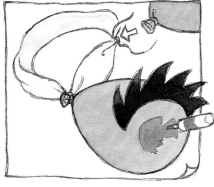

4. Draw pupils on the balloons. Use yarn to tie the eyes to a headband and slip the band over your head. Weird!

Kings, Queens, and Castles • Murder Mystery • Stone Age (Cave People and Dinosaurs) • Tropical Luau • Disco • Beach Party • Ancient Times (Greece, Rome, or Egypt) • Outer Space • Alphabet Party (each person is given a letter of the alphabet, and comes as something beginning with that letter)

Wild West

Dress as a cowpoke and have a rootin' tootin' Wild West birthday! Cut chaps out of old pants and add fringes along the sides. A bandanna, vest, hat, and boots complete the look!

Olympics

Come dressed as a gymnast, skater, or track-and-field star— and hold your own Olympic games! At the end of the party, award medals— foil-covered chocolate coins on ribbons!

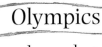

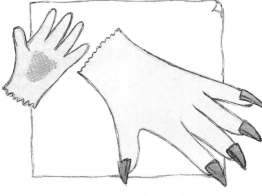

5. For monster hands, glue construction-paper nails to old gloves. Make them all different shapes and colors!

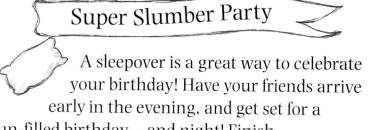

Super Slumber Party

A sleepover is a great way to celebrate your birthday! Have your friends arrive early in the evening, and get set for a fun-filled birthday—and night! Finish the party with a special birthday breakfast the next morning.

Play Mystic Mind Reader and amaze your guests—but only the Mystic and her assistant must know the secret of the game. The Mystic leaves the room, and someone is chosen to be "It." When the Mystic returns, she will astound everyone by naming the chosen person.

What's her secret? Easy—her assistant says a sentence beginning with the first letter of the person's name. For example, if Susan is "It," the assistant says, "So, great Mystic, tell us who it is." If several people have names beginning with the same letter, use the initials of the person's first and last names for the first two words of the sentence.

You can make your own food, or have pizzas delivered—let your guests choose their own favorite toppings.

No slumber party is complete without a good, old-fashioned pillow fight! Make sure lamps, plants, etc. are safely out of the way—and let the feathers fly!

After the pillow fight, calm down with a game like Rumors. One person whispers a silly rumor to the person next to her, and that person whispers the rumor to the person next to her, and so on. The last person repeats the rumor out loud—see how close it is to the original!

If the weather's good, and you have space—and a tent—why not camp out under the stars? Make sure everyone brings a sleeping bag and a pillow. You can roast hot dogs and marshmallows (with adult help, of course).

Later, after dark, you can tell spooky ghost stories late into the night. Switch off the flashlights, and see who can tell the scariest story of all! You may not get much sleep, but you'll store up enough exciting birthday memories to last all year!

Rent some videos, and make big bowls of popcorn. Then sit back, relax, and enjoy an evening at the movies!

Invitations

Send invitations early, so your guests have plenty of time to plan for your party. You can buy ready-made invitations, but it's more fun to make your own—especially if you have a funky theme.

If you only need a few invitations, you can take the time to make them elaborate. But if you need lots, you'll probably want to make them simpler. Here are a few invitation ideas for some of the themes in this book.

You will need

large sheets of paper • carbon paper • felt-tip pens, crayons, or poster paints • pencil • ballpoint pen • glue and glitter (optional) • cardboard • aluminum foil

Star Treatment

Cut a star shape out of cardboard, decorate with glitter and a cool picture of yourself. Add a stand-up tab at the back for an extra kick.

COME TO Star Sebastian's BIRTHDAY February 28th 2 p.m.

Wanted!

1. Draw a wanted poster on scrap paper. When you're sure of your design, draw it carefully in pencil on full-sized paper.

2. Lay carbon paper (dull side down) over a sheet of paper. Put your drawing on top and trace to transfer the design.

3. Repeat step 2 to make as many invitations as you need. Then just color them in, and send them to your friends!

Intergalactic Fun

Fold paper in half and draw a Martian or rocket on the front. Cut around the outlines (be sure to leave some of the folded side uncut) and decorate. To make a planet, cut out a cardboard circle and cover with aluminum foil. Write on the foil with ballpoint pen, or by pressing with the end of a paintbrush.

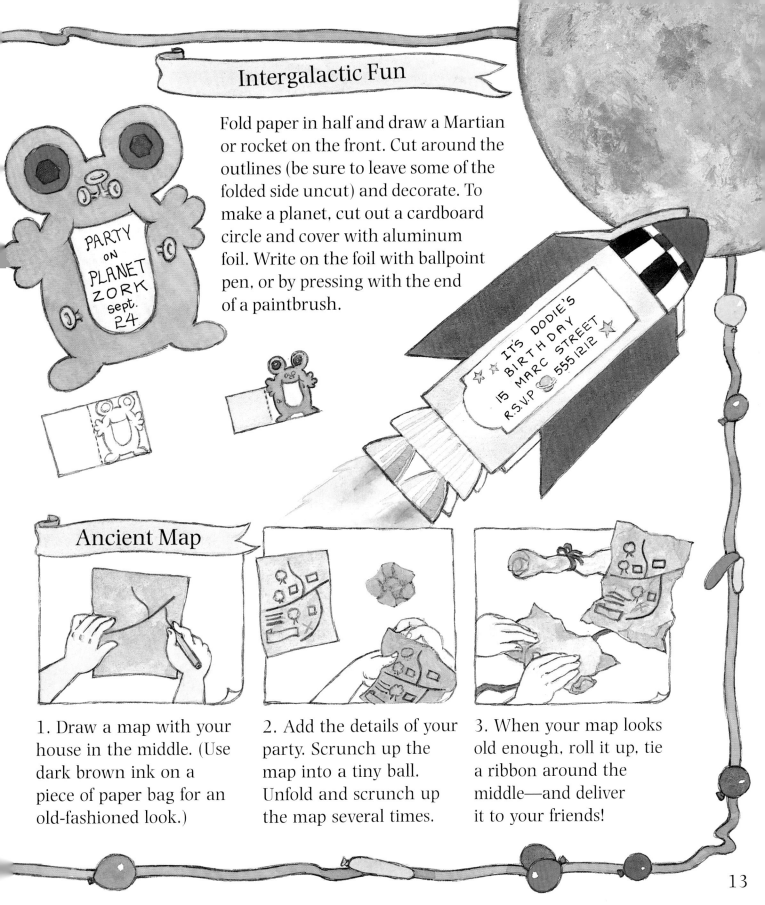

PARTY ON PLANET ZORK sept. 24

IT'S DODIE'S BIRTHDAY
15 MARC STREET
R.S.V.P 555 1212

Ancient Map

1. Draw a map with your house in the middle. (Use dark brown ink on a piece of paper bag for an old-fashioned look.)

2. Add the details of your party. Scrunch up the map into a tiny ball. Unfold and scrunch up the map several times.

3. When your map looks old enough, roll it up, tie a ribbon around the middle—and deliver it to your friends!

You will need
old magazines and newspapers
• scissors • glue • paper • felt-
tip pens or crayons

Cut out words and pictures that go
with your theme. Arrange and glue
onto paper. Make a different
invitation for each guest.

Top Secret Codes

For a mystery or secret
agent party, try writing
your message in secret
code. Your friends will
be intrigued!

Don't forget to
include a decoder key
like the one below. See if
you can decode our
message!

Pop Art

Pop-up invitations are fun to make, and even more fun to get! These instructions can be adapted for any theme.

A pop-up bird would be great for a wildlife party. You can make monsters, aliens, dinosaurs—anything!

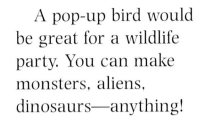

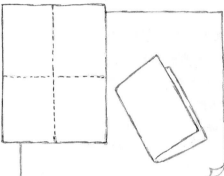

1. Start with an ordinary sheet of paper. Fold in half, then in half again to make quarters.

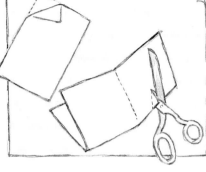

2. Make a 1/2-inch snip, then fold each side of the snip over to form two triangles.

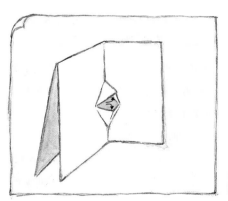

3. Put your fingers inside the card and behind the triangles. Gently push them out.

4. Decorate the invitation and add your party details. Your friends will love the surprise!

BE AN ANIMAL AT LENNY'S PARTY

LEAP AROUND AT PENNY'S PARTY

COME BE A CLOWN AT JENNY'S PARTY

Decorations

Decorations don't have to be elaborate or expensive—balloons and streamers will make any birthday celebration colorful and festive. But for a unique party, nothing beats decorations you've made yourself.

Making your decorations can be almost as much fun as the party itself. Use your theme as a guide, and plan your decorations around it. These suggestions will adapt to almost any theme—let your imagination go wild!

Tablecloths

For an exotic effect, bunch a long sheet of crepe paper around the outside of the table. Or use a plain white paper cloth, and have your guests draw designs to go with the party theme!

Place Cards

Design place cards to go with your theme. Draw stars for a Hollywood party, bats for a monster party, or animals for a wildlife party.

Mobiles

You can make simple, attractive mobiles to go with any theme. For a space party, cut stars, planets, and rockets out of shiny cardboard. For a monster party, make spooky spiders out of crumpled-up black tissue paper and pipe cleaners.

On Stage!

If you're having a Hollywood party, set up a stage and hold a talent show. Mark the stage area with masking tape, or tack down an old sheet. Arrange chairs for the audience.

Lighting

Use a desk lamp as a spotlight for your talent show. For a disco or other evening party, a strobe light or other flashing lights can be fun and exciting.

Party Food

If you're having lots of people at your party keep the food simple, so you don't have too much work to do. On the next few pages you'll find ideas for some special birthday treats you can make with only a little help. Of course, no birthday is complete without a cake, and these two are definite winners!

You will need
round cake or ring cake • frosting • sugar wafers • food coloring • ice-cream cones • assorted candy pieces (gumdrops, chocolate chips, etc.)

Monster Cake

1. Cut a hole in the middle of a round cake. Cut the remaining ring in half. (Make sure the cake is cool before it's cut.)

2. Make a snake shape, and cover with frosting—of any color! Cut sugar wafers into triangles to make monster scales.

3. Add cones for the head and tail, and decorate with candy pieces. Go wild with colors and patterns!

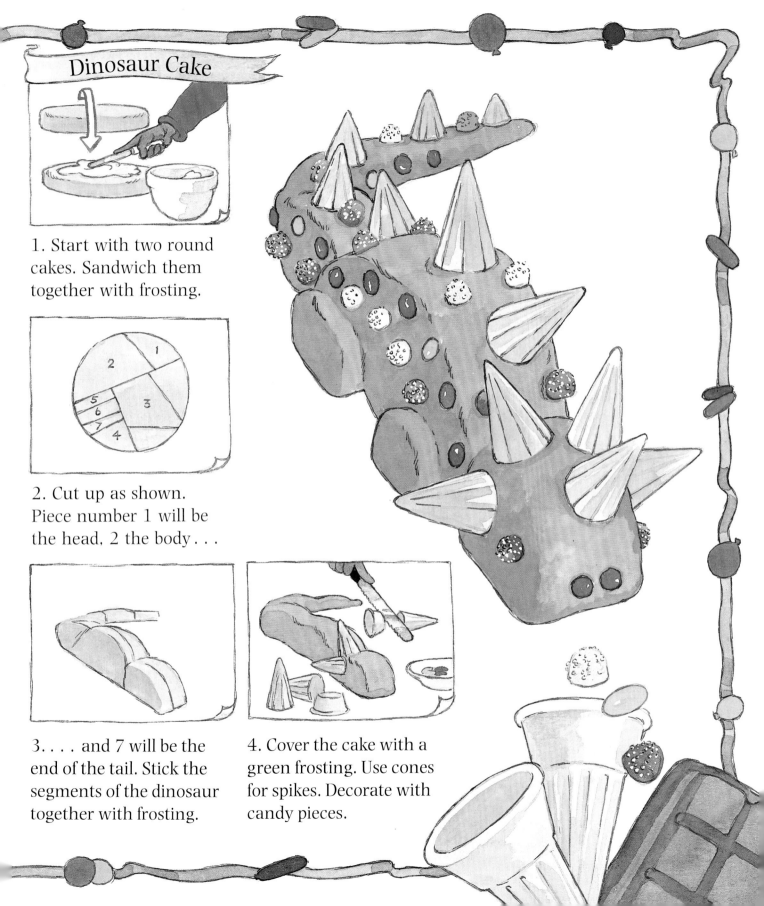

Dinosaur Cake

1. Start with two round cakes. Sandwich them together with frosting.

2. Cut up as shown. Piece number 1 will be the head, 2 the body . . .

3. . . . and 7 will be the end of the tail. Stick the segments of the dinosaur together with frosting.

4. Cover the cake with a green frosting. Use cones for spikes. Decorate with candy pieces.

Do-It-Yourself Sundaes

You will need
ice cream • cones • assorted toppings—cookies, nuts, syrup, whipped cream, fruit, chopped-up candy bars, etc. • bowls • spoons

1. Gather around and make some sundaes! Go with your theme: cones can be clown hats, cherries can be monster eyes.

2. For extra thrills, set a time limit and award prizes for first one finished, wackiest creation, and so on. Then dig in and enjoy—before everything melts!

Sickening Sandwiches

1. Carefully cut bread into weird and creepy shapes—bats, rats, monsters, etc.

2. Put in your filling, and add enough ketchup to ooze out—totally yukky! Add raisins for beady little eyes.

Eyeball Salad

You will need
large bowl • apples, bananas, oranges, pineapple, melon • grapes

1. Very carefully, peel all the grapes. Have an adult help you if you use a knife.

2. Chop up the rest of the fruit and put it in the bowl. When you add the grapes, they'll look and feel like slimy, slippery eyeballs. Guaranteed to gross everyone out— especially when you eat them!

Stained Glass Cookies

1. Beat together sugar, egg, margarine, and vanilla. Mix together baking powder, salt, and 1¼ cups flour.

You will need
1 cup brown sugar • ½ cup margarine • 1 tsp. vanilla • 1¼ cups flour • 1 egg • ½ tsp. baking powder • ½ tsp. salt • lollipop-type candies • cookie sheet

2. Next, mix everything together, adding some extra flour to dough until it reaches cookie dough consistency.

3. Refrigerate for 2 hours. Roll dough out and shape into designs. Lay flat on a greased, foil-lined cookie sheet.

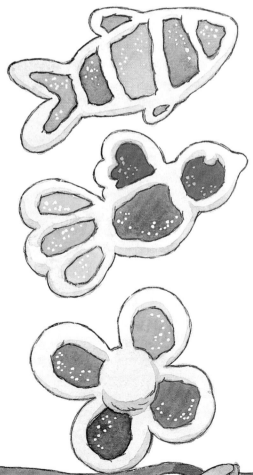

4. With an adult's help, crush candy in plastic bags with a rolling pin or a hammer. Fill cookies with different colors.

5. With an adult's help, bake at 325° for 10 minutes, or until the candy bubbles. Do not touch until cool.

Crazy Pizza

Everyone loves pizza—it's the perfect party food! It's easy and fun to make. Put toppings out in bowls. Everyone can choose his or her favorites.

You will need
pizza dough mix • spaghetti sauce • pizza toppings • mozzarella cheese • rolling pin • cookie sheets

1. Clear a large working area. Carefully follow the instructions on the box to make your pizza dough.

2. On a floured surface, roll dough out until it's ¼ inch thick. Cut and shape in zany ways! Place on greased cookie sheet.

3. With a spoon, spread the spaghetti sauce thinly and evenly over the dough. Sprinkle on grated mozzarella cheese.

4. Add your favorite toppings! With an adult's help, bake in a preheated 375° oven for 15–25 minutes.

Games and Activities

Once all your guests have arrived, it's time for the fun to begin! You can go for wild, wacky games, or quieter, more absorbing activities—or a combination. With all these ideas, everyone is sure to have a super time.

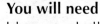

You will need
blown-up balloons • string
• rolled-up newspapers

Balloon Fight

Give each person a yard of string with a balloon tied to the end. Tie your balloon around your ankle, grab a rolled-up newspaper, and swat away! When your balloon pops, you're out. The last one with a balloon left wins!

Nose Race

1. Line up two teams. The person at the front of each line puts a matchbox sleeve on his or her nose.

2. At the word "Go," the person passes the matchbox back, using noses only!

3. If someone drops the matchbox, that team must start over. The first team to get it to the end wins!

Frame-Ups

You will need
instant camera and film
• cardboard • popsicle
sticks • white glue • paint
and brushes • scissors

1. Take instant photos of your guests. To make the frames, glue two popsicle sticks to opposite ends of a cardboard square (make each side of the square the length of a popsicle stick).

2. Glue two sticks to the ends of the first two, so all four sides of the square are covered. Repeat several times, alternating sides and top and bottom.

3. Paint the frame. When the paint is dry, slip in the photos. Your friends will have unique and lasting party favors!

Cereal Hockey

You will need
empty cereal box
• paper • scissors
• tape

1. Cut the cereal box in half. Cut an opening in each half to make goal area. Put the goal boxes at each end of a table.

2. Stick the goal boxes down with tape. Roll a sheet of paper into an "airstick" for each player.

3. Make a puck out of a piece of crumpled-up paper. Then try to blow the puck into the other side's goal box. Try not to get out of breath!

You will need
paper plates
- cellophane tape
- paper • string
- 2 chairs

Plate Tennis

1. Make rackets by taping two plates together, face to face. Leave a space just big enough for your hand.

2. Put the chairs about 5 feet apart and tie the string across them—this will be your net. To play, just hit a crumpled piece of paper back and forth across the net!

Ice Sculpture

Here's a cool idea for a hot day! Freeze water or lemonade in plastic containers ahead of time. Give your guests big plastic aprons and have them create original ice sculptures with no tools except their hands and mouths!

Hot Chocolate!

You will need
large chocolate bars • butter
knives • cutting boards

1. Divide everyone into teams. Put a bar of chocolate and a butter knife on a cutting board for each team. Line each team up in front of cutting board.

2. Go! The first person cuts a square of chocolate and passes it to the person behind, who passes it back. Meanwhile, the first person runs to the end of the line to eat the chocolate. The first team to finish its bar wins.

Talent Show

1. You act as MC—your guests provide the talent. They can sing, dance, act out a scene from a movie or TV show, tell jokes . . . whatever!

Crazy Olympics

1. Create teams of three to six people. Set up a start and finish line—most of these nutty events involve racing! You may want to set up more than one start and finish—then you can have a mayhem of events!

2. Have everyone sit down, then announce each act. You can award prizes at the end for best music, best costumes, etc.

2. Each team should be given a bucket. As each member of the team wins an event, she or he is given an apple, which should then be placed into the team bucket. The team with the most apples in their bucket at the end of the olympics wins!

3. Here are some ideas for events: leapfrog race • three-legged race • limbo • pie-eating contest • egg and spoon race • headstand contest • backward long-jump • running backward race (be careful with the backward ones!

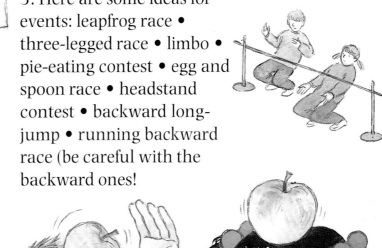

Suitcase Chase

1. Pack the wacky wardrobes into the suitcases. Divide everyone into three teams. The first player on each team picks up a suitcase and runs from the start to the finish line.

2. Put on all the clothes. Run back to starting line with suitcase, take off clothes, repack suitcase, and hand to next player.

You will need
3 suitcases • 3 each of hats, skirts, pants, socks, shoes, gloves, or anything you can think of—the crazier the better!

3. Clothes can be backwards, inside-out, or in the wrong place, as long as they're *on*. The first team to finish wins!

Tinseltown Trivia

This one requires some research—but the fun is worth it! Gather information about movie, sports, and rock stars. Once you have a list of amazing facts and pictures, make up questions. Sit your guests down and fire away!

You will need
toilet paper

Mummy Race

Divide everyone into teams of three. Give two people on each team a roll of toilet paper. At the word "Go!" these lucky people will try to wrap the third member of the team into a mummy. The first team to have a completely mummified member wins! (Be sure to leave your mummy's face free from wrap.)

T-Shirt Painting

Before you start, cover your work area with newspaper. Slip cardboard inside each T-shirt to stop paint from seeping through.

You will need
white T-shirts (1 for each guest) • newspaper • cardboard • fabric paints • paintbrushes

1. Draw your designs out on paper first.

2. Start painting! Be sure to follow the instructions.

3. Get an adult's help if you need to iron the shirt.

Pin the Mustache on the Cowboy

Draw a life-size picture of a cowboy and tack it to a wall. Cut out a heavy paper mustache for each player. Put sticky putty on the back of each mustache. Players are blindfolded, spun around, and sent off to pin the mustache on the cowboy. The one who comes closest wins!